I0750266

FINISHING LINE PRESS
www.finishinglinepress.com

MATRILINEAL

poems by

Therese Gleason

Finishing Line Press
Georgetown, Kentucky

MATRILINEAL

For my mother, Mary Jo Wolford Gleason,
and all my grandmothers

Aspects of Eve

To have been one
of many ribs
and to have been chosen.
To grow into something
quite different
knocking finally
as a bone knocks
on the closed gates of the garden—
which unexpectedly
open.

—Linda Pastan

ISBN 978-1-64662-587-1 First Edition

ACKNOWLEDGMENTS

Many thanks to the following publications in which these poems, sometimes in different versions, first appeared.

Literary Mama: "Take it Back" (now titled "Chalice")
Mass Poetry (Hard Work of Hope/Poem of the Moment): "Angel Oak"
Off the Margins: "Matrilineal" (originally titled "Lineage"), "Original Sin: The Ballad of Alice Lake," "Magdalene," "Fool's Gold," "Sanatorium," and "Domestic"
Painted Bride Quarterly: "Milk Teeth"
San Pedro River Review: "Laundry Room" (now titled "Root Cellar")
An earlier version of "Magdalene" appeared in *Limestone* and in the chapbook *Libation* (2006) published by the South Carolina Poetry Initiative.

Publisher: Leah Huete de Maines
Editor: Christen Kincaid
Cover Art: Patricia Glennon
Author Photo: Alice Pepplow of the Imagery Studio
Cover Design: Elizabeth Maines McCleavy

Order online: www.finishinglinepress.com
also available on amazon.com

Author inquiries and mail orders:
Finishing Line Press
PO Box 1626
Georgetown, Kentucky 40324
USA

Table of Contents

Eve's Kitchen

What if Eden's forbidden fruit
was a banana
hung like a crescent
from a crooked hook
in Eve's kitchen, screwed
against a wall
the color of cosmic latte:
pale and bland
as the soft flesh
inside the sunny husk.

How long would she stand there,
pondering its open-ended parenthesis:
slick yellow phallus
poised to till black earth
and already sinking into darkness,
the sweetness ripening
in her nostrils, making her mouth
water, her armpits moist
with something like fear
or desire.

Just think how delicious
the anticipation
those last few seconds
before she grabbed
the bright handle and flung open the door—
before she fell, pulling all of us
with her, into a future
where beauty and pleasure
bloom into blackness,
where we are born dying
from our first ragged cry.

The Girl Who Cried Wolf

She wasn't wicked, just young—
a woman child who didn't fit
into her burgeoning body.
Some days she danced,
or played her pipe as the sheep slept at her feet.
Other times she sat sullenly,
cursing the grass for itching her ankles,
the sheep for their oily wool,
their grating bleats and rank manure.

Maybe she grew tired
of braiding flower wreaths
to hang on their napes,
longing for her own crown,
to be swept away by a lover,
to escape
a future already materializing:
rough hands fumbling between skirts
a belly growing heavy year after year.

Or perhaps she confused her own musk
with the wolf's scent,
half asleep at dusk
waist deep in a dream,
the yellow slits
she thought she saw
just the dregs of daylight
shivering through the trees.

The first time she sounded the alarm
the village came running with torches.
The second time she shrieked
in the night, again
they flew to her rescue,
wary eyes narrowing—
not a track in sight.

The third time, no one
saw her disappear,
following the wolf into the darkness
while the sheep milled in terror,
throwing her head back,
licking blood from her paws
under the pearl moon.

The Memory of Water

When you grow up landlocked
in rolling green hills and waves
of bluegrass cresting in the wind,
the memory of water
is imprinted in the limestone
retaining wall, inscribed
like parchment in an ancient library.

They tell you millions of years ago
Kentucky lay under a warm shallow sea
teeming with corals and brachiopods,
galaxies of algae and plankton,
crustaceans with spiraling nautilus shells
drilled down by time into layers:
shale and calcite,
Paleozoic creatures
crushed like flower petals,
mineral, plant, animal, human.

Some say the native limestone attracts,
trapping ghosts in its ossified pores—
so many tiny graves
for the fossilized remains.
As a child, you scratch your name
in the spaces between their bones
with the sharp edge of a rock,
leaving a mark of your own.

Angel Oak

Great tree
teach me how to live,
to bear thousands of days and nights,
how to witness
and survive.
What your hollow eyes have seen—
how heavy your twisted limbs
outstretched in tortuous pursuit of heaven,
how sinewy your roots
mooring you to the ground.
You rest one massive branch on the earth
genteel as a proffered arm
and humble as a bended knee,
your head bowed
your face veiled
by a mantilla of Spanish moss.

Your corrugated bark
stippled with gray barnacles—
protection for woody bones,
ancient marrow, spirits
sheltering in your secret crannies.
Tree of history
tree of beauty and pain
angel of shade and shadow
shake out your leafy mane,
bless me with flecks of dappled yellow
and saltwater rain.

Matrilineal

It's happening again,
the falling dream. I plummet
through the pinhole shaft,
hurtling feet first.
I was born breech, heels
conjunct my sister's crown—
a perilous passage. I kicked her out
into the dark of the moon:
ours was a balsamic birth,
under the waning crescent.

Twinning, it's in my blood,
my family line. I teeter,
heady with retrograde legacies,
tiptoeing on ancestral fields
sown through with bones and teeth
and thrumming with blood.

I swallow the sparks
filling myself with light,
eyes like beacons
scanning black depths

and projecting the signal
from my solar plexus,
I radiate inward and outward
slipping the confines
of body and time
as though to birth a star

or most of all to be birthed by one
under the sign of the twins
ruled over by Mercury's wings,
traveling back and forth, begot
between life and death
at the speed of thought.

Inheritance

My great-grandmother's hemiplegic
migraines freezing
the left side of her body,
one eye drooping,
the other pinned open in a glazed stare.

My twin sister's wormhole
in the right headlight of her vision,
choroidal neovascularization,
monthly steroid injections
to keep the mess of blood vessels
from overtaking her sight.

My other sister's inkblot cornea
monitored for malignancy.
One brother born colorblind,
the other's left eye socket smashed—
a brick lobbed through the car window into his face

damaging the optic nerve,
leaving only a sliver of light
like a last-quarter moon
in his peripheral vision, his eyeball sunken
but intact, fully dilated
till emerald dye was inked on his retina
to shrink the pupil back to a pinhole.

How did I end up here,
keeper of the archive?
The only one to escape,
peering at family daguerreotypes
fumed with mercury vapor
as my ancestors' elemental eyes
the color of land, sea, and sky

stare through me.

Original Sin: The Ballad of Alice Lake

Who was hanged for witchcraft c. 1650

Oil of Tansy,
herb of Rue,
or Savin Juniper?
Tell me true.

On Boston Common
where the Great Elm stood,
there the hangman
placed her hood.

Mother Alice,
Goodwife Lake
swung from the tree
till her neck did break.

The minister exhorted
in her time of duress
admit to your witchcraft
but she never confessed.
They might be lenient,
they might relent,
yet Alice Lake
would not consent.

Instead she maintained
from her stinking dank cell,
I am a woman of God
in a self-made hell.
It is mine own fault
this sorry fate,
the noose that awaits me
I did create.
Before I was wed,
after carnal passion,
life bloomed in my womb
in unholy fashion,
and though with the devil
I ne'er did consort,
my own first babe
I tried to abort.

My dear girl survived
I did not succeed,
but God's righteous wrath
hath punished my deed.
Each day I must gaze
upon the sweet face
that I did once
take pains to erase.
And now my baby
lately dead
hath been appearing
in my head.
The empty cradle
sways at night,
when all is quiet
I take fright—
he cries and whimpers
with fevered moans,
that sear me deep
within my bones.
But when I search
he dissolves in dust.
The Almighty took him,
as I knew He must.
For in God's eyes
I am unworthy
and my other three children
don't deserve me.

And so Reverend Thompson
A witch I am not
yet well do I know
I have earned this lot.
I will walk to the gallows
with a penitent air,
clutching my Bible
and a lock of his hair.

To all ye about
who loiter agape
to watch my demise—
make no mistake.
The shame that you witness
is not what it seems:
I have met no demons
except in my dreams,
and way down deep
in my Puritan heart,
I have no knowledge
of Satan's dark art.

So into God's hands
I commend my spirit,
praying these words
might somehow clear it.
My soul now unburdened
nothing else left to say,
I beg you, kind Sir,
kick the ladder
away.

Fool's Gold

First it was papa,
the wild man
shoulders broad as the west,
off-kilter glance
flashing blue and brown
shuttered forever
in a pauper's grave.

He wrote letters
burned to ash
that mama never read,
words disappearing as the quill scraped
cheap paper tinged
with dust:

Grandfather did not approve.

When the telegram came
from Deadwood
Mama sat down hard
at the front door.
Her milk dried up
and Elliott Jr. wailed for days
curled fists clawing
empty air.

For weeks after, in wordless dreams
I flew, suspended
above outstretched arms
waiting to land in the warmth
of whiskey sweat tobacco
love.

But it was the end of days.
Tiny blood flowers
bloomed in my chest,
burning the fields to fallow.
At the fever's peak
they cropped my hair
like a novitiate.
It was the beginning of the end
and the end of the beginning.

Domestic

Coarse fingers
rough with work
plait ropes of hair.
Separating the waves
into three sections,
she weaves her truth
into the wisps slipping
through her hands.

Faley, she breathes,
inhaling the scent
of the girl's scalp—
remembered, longed for,
recognized.
The child's small body
drowsy and warm
leans into her chest, crushing
her starched apron.

Daughter.
She is nearly finished now.
Over, under, over, twist—
the braid coils around her heart:
a stranglehold.

Sanatorium

It all started in the big house,
my haven and curse.
There I bore her,
there I gave her away,
three years old
with a shorn head and a basket
of threadbare clothes,
washed and folded—
a mean estate, but not devoid
of dignity.
They stripped her
incinerating
her Sunday best
in a christening of flames,
scrubbed her skin, her name,
rebranding her:
Helen Harrington.

You could say
Faley died that day,
"Nellie" rising from the ashes
of her lice ridden rags,
bald as a newborn.

Almost.

If I hadn't taken
tubercular root
in my daughter's tiny lungs
etching a death's head
disguised as a cherub.
If I hadn't staked my claim
among delicate bronchial
tendrils and sprigs.

In church, Nellie sings the verse
And I will raise you up
on the last day. In response,
a whisper near her heart
intones *forgive me.*
Forever and ever
Amen.

Lives of the Saints

Who wouldn't love
the virgin martyrs:
Catherine with her spiked wheel,
Joan aflame on her stake,
Lucy who could not be burned
or defiled in the brothel,
and whose eyes were gouged out,
who gave the order for the executioner's blade
to kiss her neck with its silver edge,
perfumed milk and flowers flowing
from the wound's open lips.

In eighth grade, the nuns warned us
that sperm could swim up our thighs
in the slick secretions
seeping through underwear
wet from hand jobs and humping.
I chose Saint Therese of Lisieux,
the Little Flower,
for my Confirmation saint,
my first messy kiss
on a humid night
under a tree strung with sparkling lights.

At fifteen, my 22-year-old boss
drove me home from the pool,
stopping at his apartment
in his mother's basement
where we kissed and kissed.
He put a hand down my pants—
angel wings fluttering
between my legs,
my breath going faster and faster,
body hurtling toward an epiphany.

From then on, I became the Saint
of Everything But:
preserving my virginity
at least in name.

Years later, I saw Bernini's
Saint Teresa in ecstasy:
her head thrown back,
eyes closed, face slack,
lips parted, a smiling cupid
lifting her robe, poised
to plunge his arrow inside her.
I made a pilgrimage in Spain
to venerate her gnarled finger
in its glass reliquary,
kneeling to claim
my other namesake
and release my shame.

Magdalene

I kneel on the cold floor of the death room,
hard under my knees.
Head bowing, I pray over dust and bones.
I pray to the Magdalene,
to the prostitute I know,
Mary who knows me, forgives me.
Bless me Mary, the other Mary—
not the virgin but the whore.
I pray till the tears roll hot and steady.
I smell the perfume in her hair—
it brushes my feet and my face.
The angel voices float down the ancient stairs,
where the nuns are singing their praise
to the sinner, to the saint, to the sinner
saint, to the bones in the small silver box.

After the C-Section

Still huge with fluid, I bled into a thick pad
stuck to netted surgical panties, brain awash
in painkillers and hormones, itching all over
from morphine in the spinal injection,
my limp body rolled face up then heaved
sideways onto the table, arms outstretched,
wrists strapped in padded Velcro cuffs,
a blue curtain hung to block the view
of my midsection swabbed rusty with iodine,
the incision grinning above my shaved pubis,
the violent tugging—strangely painless—
your cry joining mine,
warm skin grazing my face
then whisked away in your father's arms
while I shook, my uterus plucked from its cavity
to remove the placenta then tucked back inside,
doctor coaxing fascia and muscles,
the sutures leaving a rickrack
of puckered skin swathed in gauze.

I couldn't sleep in the dim hospital room,
nurses in and out all night
to palpate my abdomen
and check beeping vitals. No longer
paralyzed in the morning, pain creeping in,
I had to walk: they sat me up
with firm hands at my back,
a blade of fire cutting me in two,
shuffling to the bathroom,
urethra raw from the burning catheter,
turning on the faucet, willing myself to pee,
staring down at my toenails, freshly painted
a few days before with bright red lacquer,
then the unexpected gush—I hadn't pushed
once, no contractions—that stained my inner thighs,
splattering thickly on antiseptic tile,

calling for the nurse, crying, afraid I was dying.
The kind one came, cleaned me up, held my hand,
talked calmly, helped me back to bed, stayed
as long as she could. When she left, longing
engulfed me, but the only mother in the room
was me.

The Elegist

I dowse for water
with a wise old woman.
Cool, clear fluid bubbles up
from deep underground.
I'm a pilgrim with a staff
trudging an ancient stone path.
I find a skull and grasp it,
staring into black orbits,
then shrug and keep walking,
having faced
without being broken
death, the granddaddy of anxiety
keeping my eyes wide open.

Underworlds

I speak for the dirt,
thick with red Kentucky clay,
for my ancestors' fields in Illinois and Iowa,
the victory garden in the Indiana knobs,
soil black and rich, nourished by death.
I speak for the pig turning on the spit—
noble mammal, flesh roasting golden,
for the smoke rising in the distance,
for the burning of green brush to clear the land.
I speak for the worm,
prostrate in the darkness, aerating the earth,
for the tangled roots,
thick and coiled, plaited to a heavy braid.
I speak for the DNA spiraling
in fine strands of hair plucked from the scalp,
for the cord that ties us by our belly
to the placenta in the moon-jelly sac.
I speak for the bladder and bowel,
in praise of their holy work.
I speak for the nether regions,
lawless borderlands
where the undercurrent of death
weaves its black thread,
and I speak for the sit-bones and hips:
the womb, the cervix, the purpled scar
above my pubic mound
whence three souls were pulled
from saltwater into the light.

Milk Teeth

Did you know teeth
are the only part of the skeleton
you can see?

I massage my daughter's
bottom incisors,
little nubs budding
in slobbery beds.

I have never broken a bone,
but once I cracked a tooth
with my midnight clenching.
At fifteen, they sliced tender gums
to carve my wisdom teeth
from an unyielding mandible.

In the recurring nightmare,
canines and molars,
my two front teeth
loose their grip
from wet pink moorings,
crumbling like old stucco
into stale mouthfuls.

What becomes of these chipped
offerings?

My father's dresser
rests primly against the wall,
bird's-eye maple gleaming.
In the top drawer, his keepsakes:
arrowheads, a daily missal,
the masks he wore
at our births.

Days after, his scent still
hovering, I found our milk
teeth: tiny white bells
clinking gently
in a plastic bag.

Chalice

I don't accept this cup of pain,
legacy I have regifted
against my will: this constant
parade of dark thoughts,
supplicants begging for relief.

I never realized how heavy
the yoke of reassurance,
how stifling the confessor's cassock,
the call to expiate
this hiccupping uncertainty—

I never realized how hard
it is to love me
when I'm like this.

She comes to me now,
my little daughter
with full moon eyes, sweaty
palms, and a stomach full of bees.
She carries the dark seed
sown in her tiny wrinkled brain
before she was born

Take it back,
this hypervigilance
impossible to appease
this malady
I wish I didn't
recognize.

Hymn to Darkness: Mammoth Cave

Clambering down the ladder
into the humid gloom,
my chest tightens, throat constricting.
When the trapdoor comes down—
a sliver of light receding, then gone—
I begin to hyperventilate.
I almost make them open that crack in the earth
so I can climb back up, frantic
as a drowning swimmer
kicking toward the surface from rock bottom.
But my friend holds my hand
till my breathing slows,
and I resolve to go on.
I cry the whole first hour,
silent tears hot on my face,
wriggling on my belly through crawl spaces
tight even for narrow young hips,
but as we descend deeper into the caverns
my body relaxes, hypnotized
by the trickling
sweating stone.

At the nadir,
we turn off our headlamps
and a consummate blackness falls
like a velvet curtain, blinding
our stunned, blinking eyes.
We huddle close in the heart of the chamber,
breath warm on each other's necks,
voices hushed with awe.
When the guide asks someone to sing,
the doorway of my mouth opens,
Amazing Grace spilling out in round, clear tones,
no vibrato, no artifice, just pure sound,

wordless as light
pouring from my lips into the void.
A blessing, notes glowing
like the pale, translucent cave fish:
eyeless, sightless, perfectly evolved
to glide in silvery flashes
through the black waters
they call home.

Root Cellar

Concrete covers the dirt floor
once lined with rough-hewn
barrels of carrots and potatoes,
bins of turnips and parsnips,
pungent onions strung
from the ceiling: homegrown roots
pried from their black beds
and still gritty with earth,
stockpiled to feed a ghostly brood
huddled against bitter gusts
seeping through clapboard.

I stoop to toss soiled clothes
into the stainless-steel drum,
startled by the face
reflected in the porthole
where a century ago, another mother
labored at her chores, bent low
in humid air tinged with mold
to palm dark fruit, palpating
lumpy tubers for bruise-spots,
flesh gone brown and mealy,
too spoiled for boiling.

In the shadows, damp
clings to our skin
with clammy fingers
as we stand in unison,
pausing to savor the stillness,
pressing hands to the chronic ache
at the base of the back, where hips
unstable from carrying babies
fuse uneasily with the spine,
then reach with weary arms
to grasp baskets heavy
with the steady burdens
of nature and time.

Puerta del Perdón

On the Camino de Santiago

Multitudes from all the nations
travelled the Road of Stars
some of them crawling
or barefoot in chains,
the wicked and pious alike
pounding the ground
with bruised heels, stinking
of sweat and hunger
and sin.

They bore the lost causes
on stretchers, swaddled in filthy cloaks,
scallop shells glowing
against all that black.
They bathed the sick in holy waters,
washing away months of grime.

The door of pardon is massive
wood and iron, fortified
by the prayers dying pilgrims
whispered or chanted or kept locked
in the reliquary of the heart.
These ancients made forgiveness
a door you could walk through, salvation
a shard of bone to venerate:
a laying on of hands.

Mother's Day

Wipe the table and counters first;
don't bother to collect scraps
in the palm of your hand—
let them fall
onto the faux cork linoleum
that always looks dirty.
Get the broom from the closet,
pull the chairs out, sweep
cereal, crumbs, and chips.
Go to the pantry, run the angled
straw tip under the base
of cabinets and fridge. Ignore
the magnet and dog treat
too far back to reach.
Shove bristles under rusty radiators
until you smack the pipe
coming up from the floor.
Stick out your lower lip,
blow upwards to flick
a strand of hair from your eyes.
Combine small piles
into a heap that you sweep
into the dustpan, extracting
a penny, barrette, and Lego head.
Lift the trash can's sticky lid,
a whiff of banana laced
with stale coffee grounds
and a tang of citrus wafting
from within. Dump
the debris into the bin.
Step back, survey the scene,
having swept
the face of the earth
clean, once again.

Pneuma

How to describe the wind,
air, spirit, breath of life?
How to explain the essence
perceptible only by something else:
a hemlock, say, its chevron fringe
swaying gently in the breeze
till a sudden gust descends,
thrashing its branches and fronds,
or a towering conifer
bent nearly double,
dark green crown bowed earthward,
surprisingly supple.
They say the violin is the instrument
closest in timbre and pitch to our own
but the wind boasts greater range—
I have heard its whispers and groans;
I have started awake to stormy shrieks
in the black of night, shuddering
at the shaking glass panes.
I have cocked my head
at the whistle and whoosh
like a rush of blood inside my ears—
moody beast, quixotic temperament!
I have seen the wind rip a house
from its stone foundation,
subsuming brick and mortar
into its swirling black skirts.
I have felt the wind's caress
like the cool back of a mother's hand
smoothing a feverish brow.
Is the wind mere vehicle
or sacred messenger:
carrier of seedpods and pollen
that green the earth,
the high priest we trust
to scatter the ashes of our dead.

Notes

"**Original Sin: The Ballad of Alice Lake**" was inspired by archival sources recounting the execution of Alice Lake around 1650 on Boston Common: she was hanged for witchcraft on the basis of "spectral evidence" as described in this excerpt from a letter from Nathaniel Mather, dated December 31, 1684 to his brother, Increase Mather, author of *Remarkable Providences: An Essay For the Recording of Illustrious Providences* (Boston, 1684): "Why did you not put in the story of… H. LAKE's wife, of Dorchester, whom, as I have heard, the Devil deceived by appearing to her in the likeness, and acting the part of a child of hers then lately dead on whom her heart was much set." The Reverend John Hale also described the case of Alice Lake in his book *A Modest Enquiry into the Nature of Witchcraft* (Boston, 1702):

> Another that suffered on that account some time after was a Dorchester Woman. And upon the day of her Execution Mr. Thompson Minister at Brantry, and J.P. her former Master took pains with her to bring her to repentance And she utterly denyed her guilt of Witchcraft; yet justifyed God for bringing her to that punishment: For she had when a single woman played the harlot, and being with Child used means to destroy the fruit of her body to conceal her sin & shame, and although she did not effect it, yet she was a Murderer in the sight of God for her endeavours, and showed great penitency for that sin; but owned nothing of the crime laid to her charge.

According to my (amateur) genealogical research, Alice Lake is my 10th great-grandmother on my maternal line.

"**Fool's Gold**," "**Domestic**," and "**Sanatorium**" are based on documents, stories, and oral histories collected by my maternal great-aunt Helen Reigelsberger Woelfel in *Indiana's Eva Buscher Reigelsberger, Her Ancestors, and Descendants,* self-published in Edina, MN (2013). Eva Buscher Reigelsberger was my great-grandmother on my mother's side. She was an adoptee and the daughter of an adoptee. In her book,

Woelfel traces the ancestry of Eva, whose birth mother, Helen "Nellie" Harrington Buscher, died of consumption thirteen months after Eva was born. Nellie asked her adoptive mother, Helen Klein Harrington, to raise Eva shortly before she died. Nellie Harrington Buscher (birth name Faley Baker) had herself been adopted as a young child (about age three) by Eva and John Harrington. Nellie/Faley's birth mother, Emma Bauknecht Baker, became destitute when her husband, Elliot Baker, left for the gold rush and never returned from Deadwood, South Dakota. Emma Bauknecht Baker's immigrant family of origin was impoverished and unable to help her support her two children, Nellie/Faley and an infant boy, Elliot Jr. (adoptive name George Rank), so she gave both children up for adoption to two different families. According to family stories, corroborated in the newsletter excerpted below, for a time Emma Bauknecht Baker worked as a domestic in the home of the Harringtons, visiting her daughter without disclosing to her child or her employers that she was Nellie/Faley's birth mother:

> The child's (Nellie's) mother had not revealed to the Harringtons her relationship. She often came to visit her daughter in the Harrington home. She slept with this little girl but never mentioned the fact that she (Nellie) was her own child. The mother of Nellie had another child, George, age six months, at the time of Nellie's coming to the Harrington home. He was reared by a Mrs. Rank of Lafayette. The father of these children had gone west for employment and expected to send for his wife and children, but apparently the father met with misfortune and never returned. Since the mother was unable to work and care for her children at the same time, the children were given for adoption.
>
> —"The Eva (Harrington) Reigelsberger Story," *Wetli World* newsletter (1959).

"**Magdalene**" is after the Basilica of St. Mary Magdalene in Vézelay, France, a 12th-century pilgrimage site that was also a major starting point for pilgrims walking the medieval Camino de Santiago or "Way of St. James" to the shrine of Santiago de Compostela in Spain.

"**Underworlds**" borrows the word "moon-jelly" and the repeated phrase "I speak for" from Camille T. Dungy's poem "Characteristics of Life."

"**Puerta del Perdón**" is after the "door of forgiveness," the entry to St. James Church (Iglesia de Santiago), a 12th-century temple in Villafranca del Bierzo on the medieval pilgrimage route to Santiago de Compostela, Spain: the supposed burial site of Saint James the Apostle. Sick or moribund pilgrims could receive the plenary indulgences they had set out to attain by attending mass and praying at the Iglesia de Santiago in Villafranca del Bierzo, provided they had walked far enough on the road to Santiago and could prove they were physically unable to continue on the final, arduous leg of the journey to the Cathedral of Santiago de Compostela as a result of illness or injury.

Additional Acknowledgments

I am deeply grateful for the generosity, guidance, and support of my teachers, Joseph Millar, Kwame Dawes, and Dorianne Laux, in the Pacific University MFA Program. In memoriam, I also wish to thank the poets Jane Gentry Vance and James Baker Hall, my teachers at the University of Kentucky.

Thank you to the Pacific MFA faculty, staff and students, for the gift of community. My love especially to the peaches (Kimberly Casey, Sarah Elkins, Melissa McKinstry), the witches (Tina Posner and Tink Faulise), and my roomie Sarah Sullivan.

Thank you to my Worcester poetry workshop: Jennifer Freed, Carolyn Howe, Susan Roney-O'Brien, Eve Rifkah, and Beth Sweeney. Thank you to the Stanley Kunitz Boyhood Home Summer Writing Series, where several of these poems began, and especially to Maura MacNeil, who led one of the workshops and gave the heart of this collection its first home.

Thank you to my great-aunt, Helen Reigelsberger Woelfel, for her stellar genealogical research uncovering the origins of my great-grandmother's birth parents and ancestral roots, and for writing it all down! Thank you to my grandmother, Mary "Mère Mère" Reigelsberger Wolford, for sharing stories and memories of her mother, Eva Buscher Harrington Reigelsberger. And my grandfather, Dr. Joe "Biggie" Wolford, for his memoirs and for encouraging my writing.

Thank you to my beloved parents, Mary Jo and Jack Gleason (forever in my heart), and my brothers and sisters: Caroline, Meg, Jack, and Tommy.

Gratitude and love, always, to Ed, my everything, for unwavering support. And to my children, Cleary, R.J., and Evie: my best and most beautiful creations.

Therese Gleason grew up in Louisville, Kentucky. She has lived in Madrid, Spain; Columbia, South Carolina; Washington, D.C., and most recently, Worcester, Massachusetts. Her first chapbook, *Libation* (2006), was written during several months she spent in Cape Coast, Ghana, where she participated in an archaeological dig in the village of Dominase. *Libation* was selected by Kwame Dawes as co-winner of the South Carolina Poetry Initiative Chapbook Competition. A Pushcart nominee, Gleason's poems have appeared or are forthcoming in *Plainsongs, The Worcester Review, America, New Ohio Review, San Pedro River Review, Literary Mama, Psaltery & Lyre, Halfway Down the Stairs, Painted Bride Quarterly, SWWIM Every Day, Off the Margins*, and Mass Poetry's "Hard Work of Hope/Poem of the Moment" Series. Gleason has an MFA in Poetry from Pacific University, and holds a Bachelors Degree in Spanish and Master's Degree in English from the University of Kentucky, where she was awarded the Wilhelmina Barrett Award for Poetry from the Honors Program. While at UK, she received an undergraduate research and creativity grant to walk the Camino de Santiago pilgrimage route in Spain.

She has taught English composition, creative writing, ESL, Spanish, and literacy in settings including universities, community college, adult and community education, and K-12 schools. She also spent over 12 years working in the field of educational research at the local, state, and federal level, co-writing and managing grants to develop interactive large-scale and classroom assessments designed to reduce barriers to testing and increase educational access and equity for all learners. A certified Wilson Dyslexia Therapist, Gleason currently teaches multisensory structured literacy as a reading interventionist for children with learning differences. She is a board member of the Worcester County Poetry Association, and Chair of the Advisory Board for the Worcester Clemente Course in the Humanities, an award-winning college-level seminar for highly motivated low-income adults seeking to build better lives for themselves, their families, and their communities. In her free time, she enjoys spending time with her husband, three children, and puppy, all of whom make her laugh every day.

www.ingramcontent.com/pod-product-compliance
Lightning Source LLC
LaVergne TN
LVHW051022080826
845145LV00009B/2761

* 9 7 8 1 6 4 6 6 2 5 8 7 1 *